EARTH

CURIOUS
Questions and Answers

EARTH

CURIOUS
Questions and Answers

Words by Camilla de la Bédoyère and Philip Steele

Illustrations by Daniel Rieley (including cover), Tim Budgen,
Mike Moran and Richard Watson

MILES
KELLY

First published in 2020 by Miles Kelly Publishing Ltd
Harding's Barn, Bardfield End Green, Thaxted, Essex, CM6 3PX, UK

Copyright © Miles Kelly Publishing Ltd 2020

This edition printed 2022

4 6 8 10 9 7 5 3

Publishing Director Belinda Gallagher
Creative Director   Jo Cowan
Editorial Director   Rosie Neave
Senior Editor   Amy Johnson
Designers   Joe Jones, Simon Lee, Andrea Slane
Image Manager   Liberty Newton
Production   Jennifer Brunwin
Reprographics   Stephan Davis
Assets   Lorraine King

ISBN 978-1-78989-150-8

Printed in China

British Library Cataloguing-in-Publication Data
A catalogue record for this book is available from the British Library

Made with paper from a sustainable forest

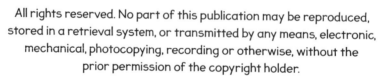

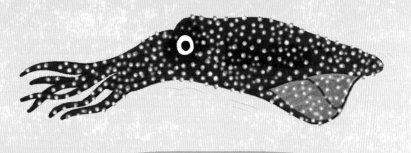

CONTENTS

OUR PLANET

What is the Earth?

The Earth is a big, blue planet that travels through space. It is the planet we live on – in fact it is full of life!

Polar bear

Animals and plants live on the land and in the oceans too!

Is there life on other planets?

Not that we know of. There are living things on Earth because there is air, water, warmth and light.

It's night time where the Earth faces away from the Sun.

Penguin

Why is it dark at night?

As the Earth travels around the Sun it spins, too. This means sunlight can only shine on one part of the Earth at a time.

South Pole

Why does the Earth need the Sun?

The Sun is a giant, hot star in space, and the Earth travels around it. The Sun gives us just the right amount of light and heat for plants to grow. Without the Sun, the Earth would be a dark and frozen planet, and nothing could live.

Is Earth like a jigsaw?

Yes, because it's made of pieces that fit together! The pieces are called plates and they are made of rock. The thickest parts of the plates poke up above the sea to form dry land, where we live.

The plates float on hot rock

The plates are always moving very slowly and creating new land, seas and mountains

How do mountains grow?

Mountains are the tallest parts of the planet. Most of them grow when one plate moves and crashes into another plate. The rocks bend and fold, making mountains.

When plates move they can create earthquakes and volcanoes

How tall is the tallest mountain?

Mount Everest is the tallest mountain, and it is 8848 metres high. Everest is part of a group of mountains called the Himalayas.

Bar-headed geese are some of the highest-flying birds. We can soar over the Himalayas.

Mountain goat

Mountains are millions of years old, but some of the rocks deep inside the Rocky Mountains could have been made more than a billion years ago!

Snow leopard

What lives on a mountain?

Nimble-footed snow leopards chase mountain goats across slippery slopes. Life is hard on a cold mountain because there is often snow all year round.

CRASH!

Moving plates smash together

Hot rock

How are rainbows made?

Although we can't see it, sunlight is made up of all the colours of the rainbow. As a beam of sunlight passes through raindrops, it is split into seven colours. This creates an arc of red, orange, yellow, green, blue, indigo and violet bands in the sky.

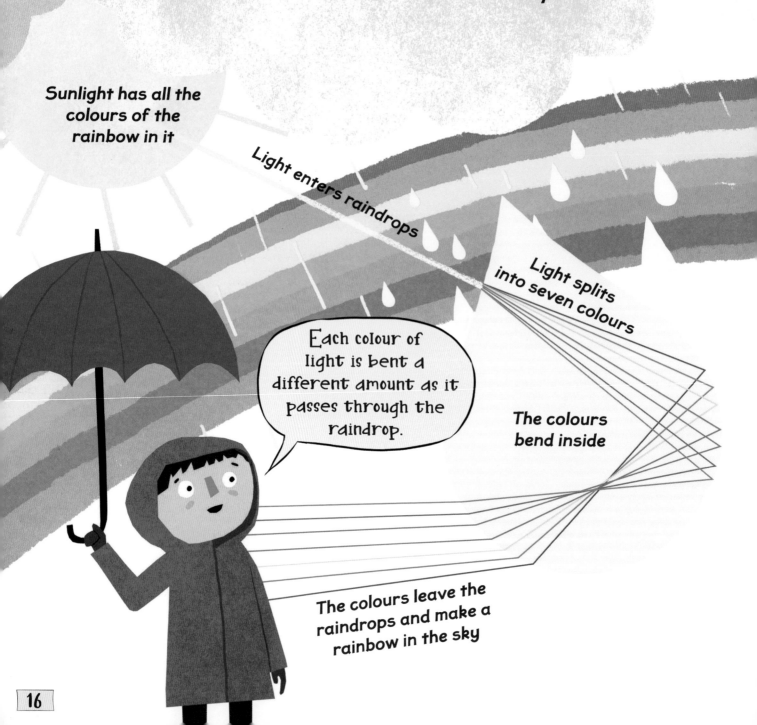

Sunlight has all the colours of the rainbow in it

Light enters raindrops

Light splits into seven colours

Each colour of light is bent a different amount as it passes through the raindrop.

The colours bend inside

The colours leave the raindrops and make a rainbow in the sky

Why does thunder clap?

In a thunderstorm, the loud noise you hear is actually caused by lightning. The air becomes so hot from the heat of electrical lightning, it expands very quickly, causing the sharp clapping or rumbling sound we call thunder.

Why is snow white?

Snow is made of lots of tiny ice crystals. When these crystals become packed together as snow on the ground, they reflect all the colours of light by the same amount. When this happens, white light is made, which is why snow appears white to us.

Snowflakes are made of ice crystals, and every one is different!

Did you know?

The loudest **thunderclaps** can shake houses and shatter glass windows.

If **Mount Everest** were at the bottom of the deepest ocean, its tip wouldn't appear above the water's surface!

More people have been to the **Moon** than have been to the deepest part of the **sea**.

The Earth's **plates** move very slowly — sometimes as little as 2 centimetres in one year.

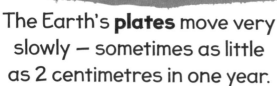

Bees can see colours in **sunlight** that are invisible to us, but they can't see red!

When **moonlight** is bright enough you might see a rainbow. It's called a **moonbow**.

Because of the way the world spins, you would weigh less if you were at the **North Pole** or **South Pole**!

If you took off in an **aeroplane** at breakfast time on Monday, and flew all around the world, you could be home for lunch on Wednesday!

We have just one **Sun**, but in outer space there are at least 200 billion more suns!

The centre of the **Earth** is hotter than the surface of the Sun.

Huge piles of bat **poo** can collect in caves where bats sleep. The poo is so smelly that the gas it gives off can kill animals that want to move in.

Big lumps of burning rock can explode out of a **volcano**, flattening anything they land on.

Planet Earth is a giant **magnet**. Animals such as bar-headed geese use the Earth's magnetism to find their way when they go on long journeys.

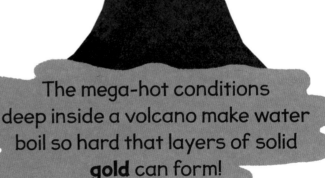

The mega-hot conditions deep inside a volcano make water boil so hard that layers of solid **gold** can form!

The Andes are the longest chain of **mountains** in the world. They pass through seven countries!

When the world's deepest lake **freezes** the ice can be more than one metre deep. Cars can drive on it!

What is the water cycle?

The way that water moves around our planet is called the water cycle. Most of the world's water is salty.

Sun

Clouds start to form

Water vapour rises

Water is all around us, even when we can't see it. It's not just in the sea and rivers. It's also in the air and in the ground.

Salty water in the ocean warms up and turns into water vapour, a type of gas. This is called evaporation. The salt stays in the ocean.

People use fresh water to drink, cook, wash, grow their crops and give to their animals.

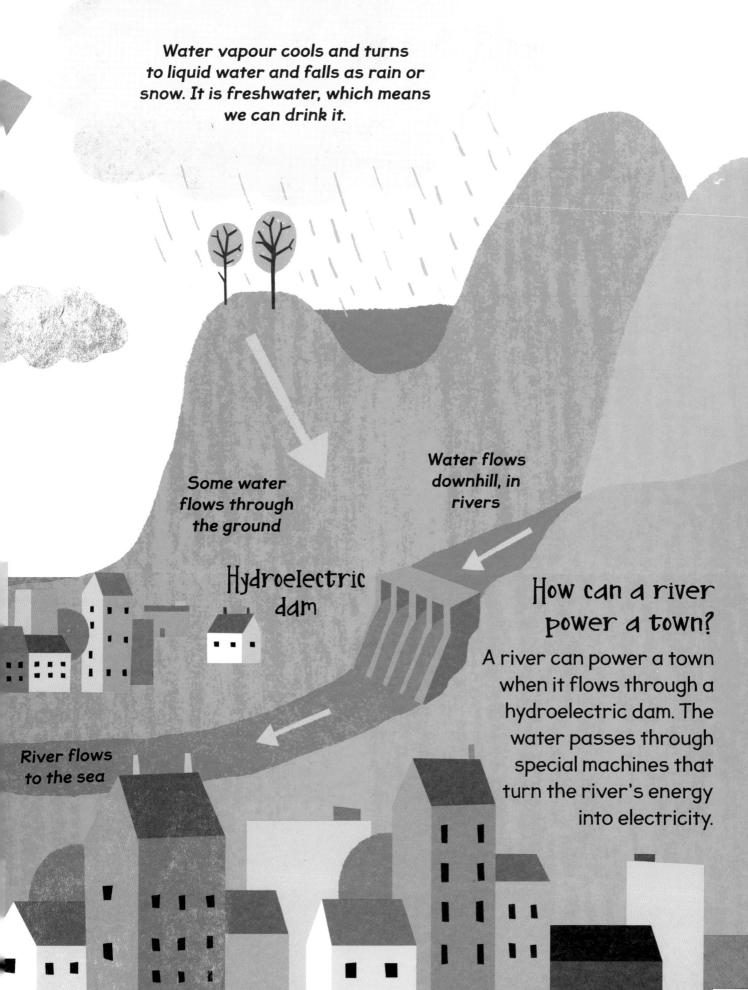

Water vapour cools and turns to liquid water and falls as rain or snow. It is freshwater, which means we can drink it.

Some water flows through the ground

Water flows downhill, in rivers

Hydroelectric dam

River flows to the sea

How can a river power a town?

A river can power a town when it flows through a hydroelectric dam. The water passes through special machines that turn the river's energy into electricity.

How many oceans are there?

There are five oceans, but they all join together to make one enormous World Ocean. Most of the Earth is covered with oceans and seas – about 70 percent!

At rocky shores, rock pools form when the tide goes out

All kinds of animals live on a coral reef

What ocean animal is both big and small?

Coral is! It's a tiny animal that builds a rocky cup around itself, but billions of them together create a living rocky reef. A reef makes a great home for other animals too!

Why is the sea salty?

Salt in the sea comes from rocks on the land. Rivers bring the salt from the land to the sea. Some salt also comes from rocks at the bottom of the sea.

I'm a parrotfish. I nibble on reefs and make sandy poo. Golden beaches are covered in my coral poo!

The water in the World Ocean is always on the move, flowing around the Earth as currents.

Wind creates waves at the surface of the ocean

I'm a green turtle. I swim across oceans to lay my eggs on a beach.

I'm a mako shark – the fastest shark in the ocean.

How deep is the ocean?

Where the ocean meets the land, it is shallow. Further away it can be very deep, dark and cold. Strange animals live there!

Fangtooth

Angler fish

What is the Equator?

The Equator is an imaginary line that cuts the Earth into two halves. Near the Equator, the weather is hot and sunny most of the time.

Arctic Circle

NORTH AMERICA

EUROPE

I am a jaguar, and I live in the tropical Amazon rainforest in South America.

The Sun shines strongly around the Equator, and there is daylight for 12 hours a day, every day.

Equator

SOUTH AMERICA

I am an emperor penguin and I live on frozen Antarctica with lots of other penguins, seals and birds. This is the coldest place on Earth!

Where does the Sun shine at midnight?

During the summer months in the far north of the world, the Sun doesn't set. In places such as Canada, Alaska, Russia, Greenland, Norway and Sweden the Sun can be seen in the sky at night. But in winter it is cold and dark all the time.

I'm a polar bear, and I live in the far north on the Arctic ice. I love eating seals!

I'm a tiger and I love the rain. I live in tropical forests of India, and I'm a very good swimmer.

ASIA

AFRICA

What is a rainy season?

Tropical places near the Equator are hot and humid. Strong winds called monsoons bring wet weather in summer. This is called the 'rainy season'.

OCEANIA

ANTARCTICA

How many?

24
The number of hours in a day... because it's the number of hours it takes for the Earth to spin once.

365
The number of days in a year.

About **50** volcanoes erupt every year on Earth.

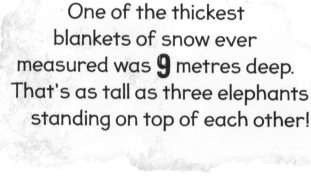

One of the thickest blankets of snow ever measured was **9** metres deep. That's as tall as three elephants standing on top of each other!

The sea freezes over near the North Pole in winter. The ice can be more than **3** metres deep in some places.

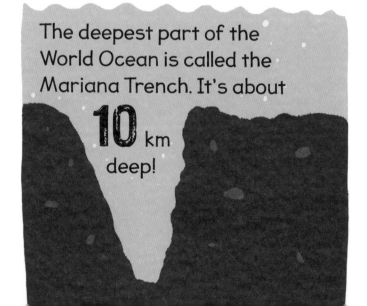

The deepest part of the World Ocean is called the Mariana Trench. It's about **10** km deep!

2 The number of summers enjoyed by Arctic terns every year. These white birds fly all the way from the Arctic to the Antarctic to get the best weather!

In one year, **10,000** millimetres of rain can fall in a tropical rainforest, while less than one millimetre falls in the driest deserts.

It takes about **1000** years for a drop of water in the World Ocean to flow once around the Earth.

1.3 million Earths could fit inside the Sun.

In the Antarctic, around the Earth's South Pole, temperatures can drop to **−50°**Celsius, or even lower.

Earth is about **4.5 billion** years old.

In the last **50** years about one third of all Earth's rainforests have been cut down.

No one knows how many different types of animal there are on the planet, but it could be as many as **10 million.**

Are all deserts hot?

No, a desert can be hot or cold, but it's a dry place because it rarely rains. More rain falls in the hot and sandy Sahara Desert than in Antarctica, which is a frozen, windy desert that's covered in snow!

Pillar

Arch

Hoodoos

Why do desert rocks look so weird?

The wind picks up desert sand, and blasts it against the rock. Over time it carves out some amazing rock shapes such as hoodoos, pillars and arches.

Why do I need such big ears?

Those big ears help a fennec fox lose excess heat in the Sahara Desert. They're also good for listening out for burrowing bugs under the sand.

Why don't penguins get frostbite?

A penguin's body is suited to life at the Antarctic. Its thick feathers are like a waterproof blanket, and warm blood travels through the bird's feet so they don't freeze.

Penguins hold their eggs on their feet to keep them warm

Oasis

What's an oasis?

An oasis is a place where water can be found in a hot desert. It's one of the few places that plants can grow.

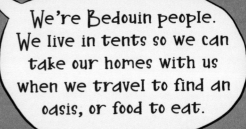

We're Bedouin people. We live in tents so we can take our homes with us when we travel to find an oasis, or food to eat.

Does it rain every day in a rainforest?

It can do! Rainforests are found in tropical areas around the Equator. The Amazon Rainforest is the largest rainforest in the world. It's in South America and is home to millions of animals and plants, from tiny ants to giant trees.

Monkeys and parrots feast on the tropical fruits

Why are plants important?

Animals need plants to survive because plants make oxygen. It's in the air, and we breathe it. Plants are also food for us and many other animals. When plants die they rot and turn into soil, which we use to grow more plants.

Rainforest plants have giant leaves and they grow flowers all year round.

The forest floor is home to fungi, frogs and billions of ants and other bugs

Trees grow tall and straight to reach the sunlight

It can be noisy in a rainforest. Birds sing, insects buzz, and howler monkeys like me call and whoop to each other!

Lizards and snakes hunt insects

Silent jaguars creep through the dark shadows or hide high up on branches

Morpho butterfly

Lianas are climbing plants that have long, bendy stems and dangling branches

Would you rather?

Would you rather search for aliens in **space**, or travel to the bottom of the **sea** and discover freaky fish?

If you were frozen water, would you prefer to be a **snowflake** or an **icicle**?

Would you prefer to be as tall as a **mountain**, or as colourful as a **rainbow**?

Would you rather swing like a **monkey** or swim like a **fish**?

What type of boat would you like to be in right now...

...a canoe on the **Amazon River** or a sailing boat on the **Atlantic Ocean**?

Would you prefer to dig for **diamonds**...

... or **dinosaur** bones?

If you lived somewhere else would you prefer to live in the desert like a **fennec fox**, or in the Arctic like a **polar bear**?

If you could be a plant would you choose to be a giant **rainforest tree** or a prickly **cactus**?

What do we get from the Earth?

We get lots of things from the Earth! They are called natural resources. Animals and plants are used for food and clothing. We use metals and other minerals to make things. We can even use wind and water to give us power.

Plastics are strong and waterproof. They are often made from oil, which comes from the remains of tiny animals that once lived in the sea.

Glass is made from sand

My bike is made of different materials that are found on Earth.

Rubber is a bendy, stretchy material that comes from rubber trees

Rocks are made of different materials called minerals. Metals such as gold and silver are minerals. Most sand is a mineral called quartz.

Metal

Fossil

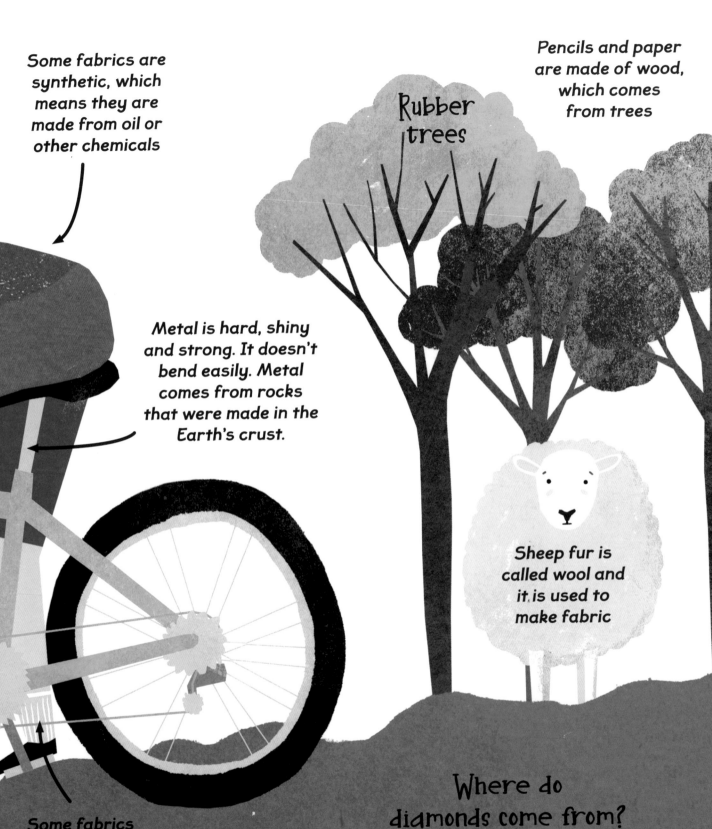

Some fabrics are synthetic, which means they are made from oil or other chemicals

Metal is hard, shiny and strong. It doesn't bend easily. Metal comes from rocks that were made in the Earth's crust.

Rubber trees

Pencils and paper are made of wood, which comes from trees

Sheep fur is called wool and it is used to make fabric

Some fabrics are natural and they are made from plants or animal fur

Diamonds

Where do diamonds come from?

Diamonds are a type of mineral that forms deep below the Earth's crust. Diamond is the hardest natural material, but it can be cut to make sparkly precious crystals or 'stones'.

Why does Earth need our help?

We are doing lots of damage to our planet!

We chop down too many trees. But trees make oxygen for us to breathe, and are home to many animals.

We poison the oceans with waste. Coral reefs and animals die in dirty water.

We pollute the atmosphere. Dirty air is making our planet too warm.

So what can YOU do about it?

Recycle your rubbish instead of throwing it away.

Turn off water when brushing your teeth.

Let your computer sleep instead of screensaving.

Don't leave chargers plugged in at the wall.

Pick up litter!

Plant trees!

Get involved!

Happy Earth Day!

On 22nd April every year, people across the world take part in activities to help make our planet a greener place.

A compendium of questions

Why don't we fall off the planet as it spins through space?

Thankfully, a special force called gravity keeps us on the Earth. It's a type of 'pull' force and the Earth, being heavier than us, pulls us towards its centre.

How does walking help the Earth?

Most cars and buses use fuel made from oil to power their engines. They make air pollution, so it's best to walk, or cycle if you want a healthy planet.

Can cars run on chocolate instead of petrol?

Yes! Chocolate comes from cacao trees and it can be turned into a type of fuel called biofuel. Biofuels are cleaner than petrol, so that's good news (but a terrible waste of chocolate!).

Why did my bike go rusty?

Bikes are made with a metal called iron. If iron gets wet (when it rains) the oxygen in the water joins with the iron to make a new material called iron oxide, or rust.

Rust is an orange-brown colour

Can snakes live in the Antarctic?

Most of us live in hot, tropical places.

There are no snakes in the Antarctic — snow and ice make it too cold. Snakes keep their bodies at the same temperature as the air around them, so they would freeze to death. They need warmth!

Why do planes fly above clouds, not below them?

When planes fly, air pushes against them as they move forward. This is air resistance. Air is thinner above the clouds, so there's less resistance, making it easier to fly, and so use less fuel.

Will the Earth last forever?

Earth has been around for 4.5 billion years already but it's still very young for a planet, so there's no need to panic!

I'm still just a teenager planet!

How do people travel to the deep oceans?

Explorers and scientists use special underwater ships called submersibles to travel thousands of metres down. Only three people have ever reached the deepest point, in the Mariana Trench.

What is a tsunami?

It's a giant wave that hits land and destroys everything in its path. At sea, the tsunami isn't too high, but as it nears land, the wave may be 30 metres high. It's caused by an earthquake under the seabed.

Early warning systems allow people to reach safe areas, away from the coast, before the tsunami arrives

What time is it at the North Pole?

It can be any time you like! During the deep winter there is no day, and in the middle of summer there is no night, so 'time' doesn't mean the same thing at the Poles!

Always time for ice cream though!

Are there mountains under the sea?

Yes, huge mountains called seamounts. They are formed by undersea volcanoes erupting. The waters around them attract many different sea creatures as there is plenty of food.

How big is an ocean?

There are five oceans and they are all HUGE! Together, they cover two thirds of Earth's surface.

An ocean is a large area of salty water. It's also called the sea.

NORTH AMERICA

ATLANTIC OCEAN

PACIFIC OCEAN

SOUTH AMERICA

Seaweeds are plants that live in salty water.

Day octopus

SOUTHERN OCEAN

Long-snouted seahorse

Are the oceans important?

Yes, billions of animals and plants live in them! People use the things that live in the ocean for all sorts of things, too. A type of seaweed called red algae is used in peanut butter — it makes it easy to spread!

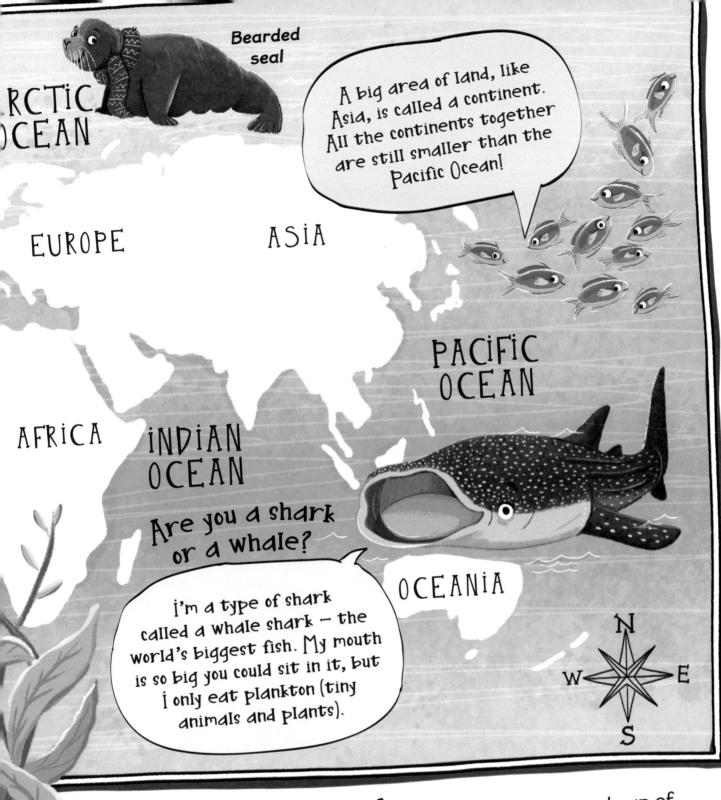

Bearded seal

RCTIC OCEAN

A big area of land, like Asia, is called a continent. All the continents together are still smaller than the Pacific Ocean!

EUROPE

ASIA

PACIFIC OCEAN

AFRICA

INDIAN OCEAN

Are you a shark or a whale?

I'm a type of shark called a whale shark — the world's biggest fish. My mouth is so big you could sit in it, but I only eat plankton (tiny animals and plants).

OCEANIA

N
W   E
S

Why is the sea blue?

Sunlight is made up of lots of colours. When it shines on the ocean, most of the colours disappear into the water, but blue light bounces back, so the ocean looks blue.

What is a fish?

Fish are animals that have skeletons, gills and fins. There are more than 32,000 types, and most of them live in oceans.

Tail fin swishes from side to side when swimming

Overlapping scales are smooth and slippery

Herring

Slim, sleek body moves quickly through water

i'm the perfect shape for swimming. My silvery scales help water to flow easily over my skin.

Can people breathe underwater too?

No – sorry! You need to breathe air because you have lungs. All fish have special organs called gills that work in water.

Water and air have oxygen gas in them. All animals need oxygen to live.

Oxygen-rich water flows in

Triggerfish

Water flows out over the gills, where the oxygen passes into the fish's blood

Do fish have special homes?

Some do. Clownfish live among the tentacles of stinging sea anemones. The fish are covered in special slime that protects them from stings, but animals that might want to eat them can't get close!

I can glide for up to 200 metres.

Can fish fly?

No – but some can glide. Flying fish have very streamlined bodies and use their big fins to launch out of the water into the air.

Whoosh!

How is my nose like a shark?

Most fish skeletons are made of bone. Shark skeletons are made of cartilage, which is softer than bone. Our noses and ears have cartilage – that's why they're bendy!

Bull shark

Did you know?

A **hairy frogfish** is a fast eater. It sucks food into its mouth like a vacuum cleaner – 50 times faster than the blink of an eye!

At 3 metres long, the ocean **sunfish** is one of the world's biggest bony fish.

Octopuses can turn red when they are angry.

Electric rays can zap fish with an electric shock. Once the fish has been stunned, the ray can eat it!

Seaweed is often used as a thickener in ice cream!

The **sperm whale** has the biggest brain on the planet – and probably the whole Universe!

500 million years ago the only living things on Earth were in the ocean.

Baby sharks and baby seals are called **pups**, and baby fish are called **fry**.

Shark skin feels like sandpaper. It is covered in tiny bumpy scales that help them slip through the water.

I'm more like a hippo than a herring!

Whales and **dolphins** aren't fish — they are mammals.

A **great white shark** can eat enough meat to make 3000 burgers in one go, and it won't want to eat again for at least ten days.

North Pole

Polar bears and **penguins** never meet because penguins live near the South Pole and polar bears live near the North Pole!

It's like looking in a mirror!

South Pole

Sailors used to think that **dugongs** were mermaids. They're actually plump mammals that spend their time grazing on sea plants.

Do trees grow in the deep sea?

No — but giant kelp seaweed grows in huge forests! It is found in the Pacific Ocean, and can grow up to 50 centimetres in one day.

Bumps contain air that helps the kelp to float

A kelp forest is a great place to hide — one strand can be more than 30 metres long.

We are lizards that live on the Galapagos Islands in the Pacific Ocean.

Who picnics at the bottom of the sea?

Marine iguanas do! They dive to depths of 12 metres — and stay there for up to an hour while they nibble on seaweed that grows on the seabed.

Do baby fish go to nursery?

Young fish and reptiles keep away from predators in special hiding places called nurseries. Shallow waters around sea grasses and mangrove tree roots make good nurseries.

Sea otters can wrap themselves in kelp so they don't float away

Mangrove trees grow at the coast, with their roots in shallow salty water.

Sea creatures sometimes mistake plastic floating in the ocean for food. If we eat it, it can kill us.

What do turtles eat?

Green sea turtles feast on fields of sea grasses that grow underwater.

Baby turtles hide from sharks in the sea grasses

Who plays hide and seek?

Many ocean animals do! On coral reefs, millions of sea creatures live close together. Lots of them use clever tricks to avoid being eaten by the others.

I look like seaweed. I'm a type of fish called a leafy seadragon.

I'm a sea slug – aren't I beautiful? My lovely colours tell animals that I am poisonous.

I'm a decorator crab, and I'm holding onto a piece of coral as a clever disguise.

I'm a cuttlefish and I can change colour in a flash.

Do fish need friends?

My best friend is a busy little shrimp. I'm a coral grouper and my friend cleans my teeth.

I also nibble away any dead skin. Yum!

We moray eels have long, thin bodies and can hide in cracks in the coral. We eat almost anything we can catch.

Can you see a reef from space?

Yes! The Great Barrier Reef stretches over 2000 kilometres off the coast of Australia. Reefs are built by tiny animals called polyps. Each one lives in its own rocky cup, waving its tentacles in the water.

It took thousands of years for polyps like me to build the Great Barrier Reef.

How long does it take to make an island?

If a volcano erupts on the seabed, it can make an island in a few years! Lava (a type of liquid rock) pours out and builds up to create a brand new island.

Volcano erupts on seabed

A cone shape of lava forms on the seabed

The cone grows so big it breaks the surface – it's a new island!

Can I find treasure on an island?

Yes – but not the sort that belongs to pirates! The treasure to be found on islands is all the precious animals that live on them.

We're baby hawksbill turtles. Our mum laid eggs in a nest and then swam away. Now we're hatching.

We're leaving our nest and heading to the sea.

I fly to islands when it's time to build my nest and lay eggs. I'm an albatross, and I'm huge.

Black and white ruffed lemur

Christmas Island, near Australia, swarms with millions of red crabs. We lay our eggs in the sea.

Who lives on an island?

Islands are often home to animals that live nowhere else on Earth. About 60 types of lemur live only on the island of Madagascar, which is in the Indian Ocean.

Giant tortoises like me are found on coral islands in the Indian Ocean. We can live to be more than 100 years old!

How many?

About **100 million** sharks are killed by people every year.

I'm one of the longest animals ever!

10 metres The length of a bootlace worm.

400 million

The number of years that sharks have lived in the oceans.

There are more volcanoes under the sea than on land! **452** are on the edges of the Pacific Ocean.

Pufferfish have poisonous flesh. About **30** people die every year after eating them.

7 metres

The length of the biggest saltwater crocodiles.

A single one of my teeth can be more than 10 centimetres in length!

A starfish can have more than **30** arms!

My arms are covered with hundreds of tiny feet. I use them to walk on the seabed.

There were **40 million** crabs on Christmas Island — until yellow crazy ants arrived. They spray the crabs with acid and eat them, so far killing about **15 million** of them.

40,000

507

...the incredible age in years of a clam that was found in the Atlantic Ocean.

Phew!

...the number of eggs a herring can lay in one go.

A narwhal's giant tooth can reach **3 metres** in length.

350
The number of types of coral that live in the Great Barrier Reef.

That's why it's important to cut down the amount of plastic you use, and to recycle it.

1 million
seabirds are killed every year by plastic rubbish that is in the ocean.

Who sleeps in a muddy bed?

Sea cucumbers do! These slug-like animals live in mud, eat mud and poo mud! Sea cucumbers are animals, not vegetables, but some people do like to eat them!

I'm a longnose sawshark. I hunt fish and crabs that are hiding in the mud. My nose is lined with sharp teeth!

The bottom of the sea is covered in mud and sand. It's called the seabed!

How do people explore under the sea?

People can't breathe in water, but we still find ways to explore the deep ocean. We can scuba dive, use submarines, or send robots with cameras.

I'm a glowing jellyfish called a mauve stinger.

Remotely operated underwater vehicles are one way for people to explore deep water from the safety of the surface

Who stands on three legs?

Tripod fish have three long, leg-like fins to stand on the seabed. Each fin-leg can be more than 50 centimetres long! Then they keep their mouths open and wait for food to swim right in.

Who lights up the deep, dark sea?

Sunlight can't reach the bottom of the deep sea. So some animals make their own light instead!

Viperfish like me use flashing lights to attract little animals to swim close. Then we swallow them up! My mouth is so big I can swallow animals bigger than me!

59

Puffin

Why does the sea go in and out?

Over the course of a day at the seaside you will see the sea moving in and out. This is called the tide, and it's caused by the Moon!

When the tide is in, the shore is covered with water. When the tide is out, there's still some water left in rock pools. How many animals can you see living here?

Eel

Brittlestar

Goby

Why is there jelly in a rock pool?

Hermit crab

I'm not jelly, I'm a beadlet anemone! When the tide is in, my tentacles wave in the water. When it goes out I fold my tentacles in so I look like a wobbly blob!

Who loves to surf?

Humans – but dolphins ride the waves too! Flat water turns to waves when wind blows over the top of it.

Which animals go to school?

We do! Young orcas like us have to learn to catch our lunch! Our mums take us to shallow water to show us how to hunt shoals of fish, seals and baby whales.

Lumpsucker

Who snacks at the shore?

Grey seals feed on all kinds of animals near the shore, from crabs to seabirds. They can also dive to depths of 70 metres when hunting.

Would you rather?

Which would you prefer — soaring with a **sea eagle** or surfing with a **penguin**?

I soar on 2-metre-wide wings, plucking sea snakes and turtles out of the water.

I use my wings like flippers to swim and leap through the waves.

My big mouth is full of eggs! After my mate lays them I keep them safe in my mouth until they hatch.

Would you rather be covered in spikes like a **pineapplefish** or have a huge mouth like a **jawfish**?

Would you rather be a **marine biologist** and study ocean animals, or a **marine geologist** and find out all about the mysterious seabed?

Would it be nicer to hold hands with a furry **sea otter**...

... or with a **blind hairy yeti crab**?

Is it better to have your feet nibbled by a **cleaner fish**, or tickled by a **feather duster worm**?

Would you rather have teeth as big as a **walrus's tusks**, or a long nose like a **sailfish**?

i'm the size of an elephant and consume 200 litres of milk a day!

...or as little as a **mother octopus**?

Would you like to eat as much as a **baby blue whale**...

i don't eat anything while i look after my eggs — and that can take eight months!

Who walks on water?

Polar bears do. They live in the Arctic Ocean. It's so cold there that the ocean freezes over.

Walruses and seals use their flippers to scoot over the Arctic ice before diving into the sea.

Why don't fish freeze?

Icefish have special blood that doesn't freeze — even if the water around them turns to ice!

Greenland sharks like me swim slowly to save energy in sub-zero temperatures.

Why do icebergs float?

Icebergs are made of frozen water. Ice is lighter than water, so it floats. Big sheets of ice float on the sea too. They are good places for penguins and seals to take a nap when they are tired of swimming, slipping and sliding!

Where did that seal go?

Under the ice — I'm brilliant at holding my breath! We Weddell seals only have to poke our heads up through holes in the ice once an hour to get air.

Who sings beautiful songs in the cold sea?

I do! I'm a white beluga whale and I sing so loudly that people in boats can hear my lovely songs.

Who packs a powerful punch?

I'm only the size of your foot, but I can smash a thick sheet of glass.

A peacock mantis shrimp is one of the world's strongest animals for its size! It uses its club-like legs to wallop other animals at lightning speed.

Sting!

Which fish has the most vicious venom?

I do! I'm an Indian stonefish. I have 13 sharp spines on my back to inject the venom, and it's strong enough to kill a human. I use this clever trick to protect myself from attack.

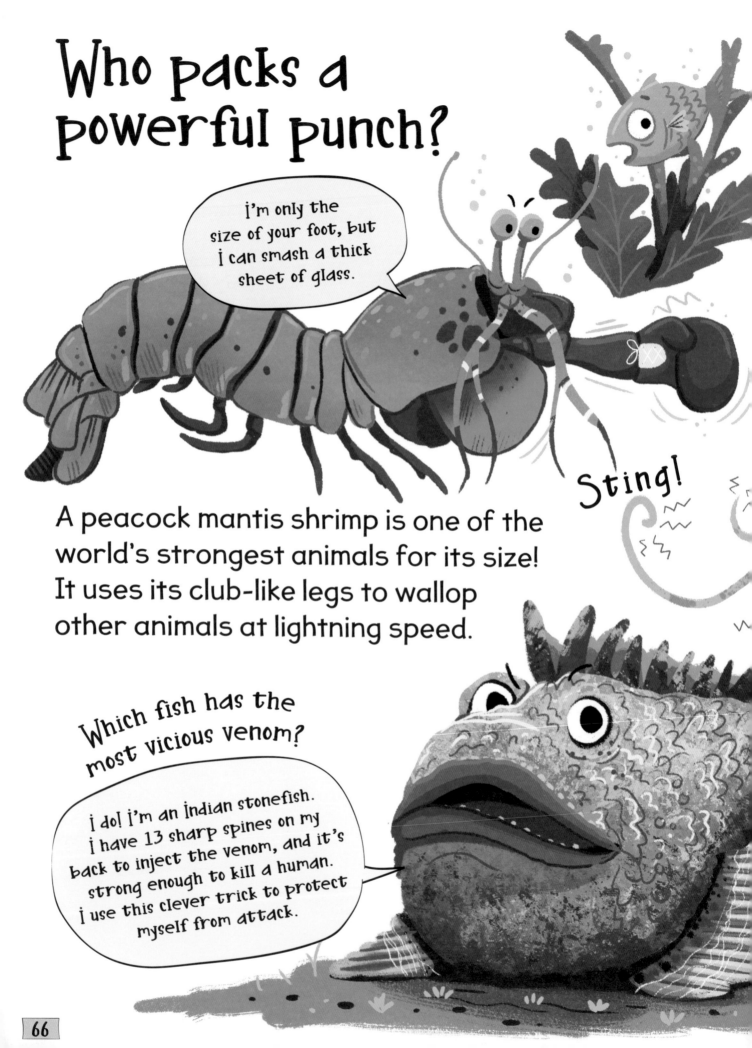

Why do jellyfish sting?

A jellyfish uses its long, stinging tentacles to get a meal. Each tentacle carries tiny, venomous darts that jab passing fish prey.

I'm a box jellyfish — the most dangerous jellyfish in the world. I have enough venom to kill 60 people!

Who can smell a drop of blood in the sea?

Sharks can! These incredible hunters have a super sense of smell that helps them find fish and other animals to eat.

Sniff!

Hammerhead sharks have strange heads. This odd shape helps us to see and smell animals, and to swim fast.

One tentacle can grow more than 20 metres long!

Are there monsters in the sea?

There are some very big animals in the sea... but no monsters. From huge rays and outsize crabs to the biggest animal on Earth – plenty of giants lurk in the deep.

Why do whales spout water?

That's how they breathe! Whales breathe air. They all have one or two blowholes, which are like nostrils. A spout from a whale is really just a big, warm, wet breath!

Which crab has the longest legs?

A Japanese spider crab has 10 legs, and each leg can be over 2 metres long! These mega crabs can reach 100 years old.

What's the biggest animal?

Me! I'm also the biggest animal to ever live! I can grow up 25 metres long and my tongue weighs the same as an elephant.

Could you sink a ship?

Giant manta ray

No! Sailors used to think fish like me could pull a ship under the water. They even called me devil fish! It wasn't true – I'm huge (up to 7 metres wide) but harmless.

Giant octopus

Blue whale

Who can reach you from 4 metres away?

Me! My eight arms are each 4 metres long, with more than 200 strong suckers on each one.

69

A compendium of questions

Can i swim across an ocean?

i swim very long distances from my feeding areas to the beach where i lay my eggs.

No human has ever swum across one without taking a break in a boat. But whales, sharks and turtles can!

The upper lobe of a thresher shark's tail fin can be as long as the rest of its body!

Why do thresher sharks have such long tails?

They use the enormous upper lobes of their tail fins to wallop shoals of their fish prey.

Which fish ties itself in knots?

A hagfish! It's covered in slippery slime and ties itself in knots when it is feasting on dead animals at the bottom of the sea.

Tying myself in a knot can also help me wriggle free of a predator.

How smart is an octopus?

An octopus can work out how to open a jar to reach food inside! It uses its suckers to grip shellfish and rip them open.

Can I drink seawater?

No — it can make you sick. Seawater is too salty, and often dirty too. The dirt is called pollution and it's bad for all living things.

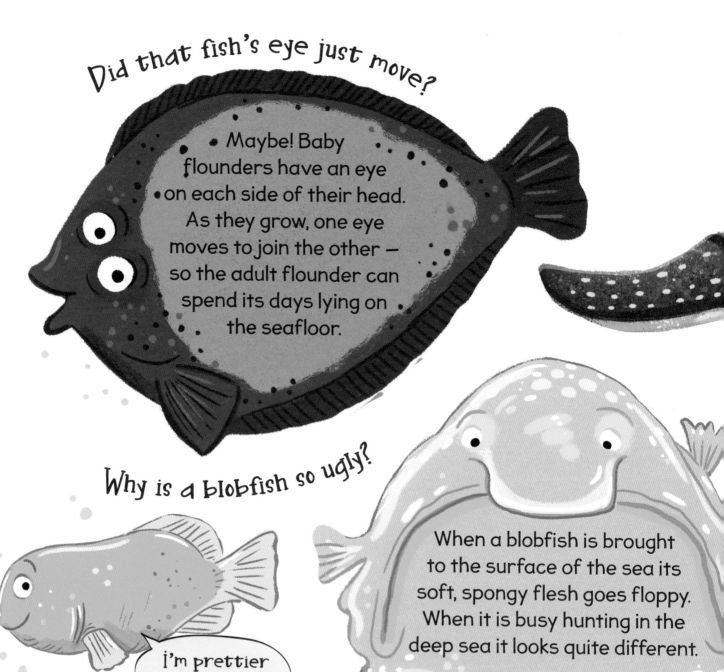

Did that fish's eye just move?

Maybe! Baby flounders have an eye on each side of their head. As they grow, one eye moves to join the other — so the adult flounder can spend its days lying on the seafloor.

Why is a blobfish so ugly?

I'm prettier underwater!

When a blobfish is brought to the surface of the sea its soft, spongy flesh goes floppy. When it is busy hunting in the deep sea it looks quite different.

I live at great depths, so humans very rarely see me!

Which fish uses oars?

The fins of the strange, ribbon-like oarfish look a bit like oars. It's the longest bony fish — reaching up to 11 metres.

Do all sharks have big teeth?

No – a whale shark can have more than 3000 teeth in its giant jaws but each tooth is tiny! They eat plankton and little fish.

Why does a firefly squid glow?

To hide, and to be seen! This squid can mimic the light above or below it if it wants to hide, and glow brightly when it wants to attract a mate.

Special organs all over the body make light

Are you scared of thunder?

What is your favourite thing to do on a sunny day?

WEATHER

What is the best thing about where you live?

What is your favourite colour?

What name would you give to a hurricane?

What is weather?

Earth is surrounded by a layer of air called the atmosphere. The way the atmosphere behaves is always changing. It is these changes that give us the weather, which may be hot, cold, wet, windy or sunny.

Sun

Earth

Mind the wind doesn't blow your hat off!

The atmosphere is filled with moving air and clouds

South Pole

Why does weather happen?

The Sun is the nearest star to Earth. It is far, far away in space, but its incredible heat warms our planet. This warmth affects the way that air presses against Earth's surface. Differences between cold and warm places create strong winds, as well as currents in the oceans.

Why do seasons change?

As Earth travels around the Sun, it is tilted. This means that northern and southern parts lean towards to the Sun at different times of the year. So when the north part is leaning towards the Sun it is summer there, and winter in the southern part.

Tilted Earth

Sun

Summer in the north

Winter in the south

North Pole

We call the weather conditions recorded over many years the CLIMATE.

Equator

Is weather important?

Yes it is, because people, animals and plants need sunshine, warmth and water to stay alive. However, extreme weather conditions, such as storms or floods, can put lives in danger.

Rain and sunshine help us make food. Then insects help new plants to spread.

What makes water wonderful?

Water is a liquid. It can freeze to become solid ice. It can turn into a gas called water vapour. Water may change its form, but it lasts forever.

2 It gets gassy

Heat from the Sun turns water into a gas, called water vapour. This is **evaporation**.

1 There's lots of it!

Over **two thirds** of the Earth's surface is covered in water.

Water is precious

Fresh water keeps us **alive**. Water helps plants grow, too. We can wash in it, swim in it, sail on it, and play in it!

Whoosh! Splash!

3 It rises and cools

As warm water vapour rises, it cools down. It **condenses**, turning back into liquid.

The higher you go, the colder it gets!

4 It makes clouds

Water droplets or solid ice crystals gather around specks of dust and form **clouds**.

5 It falls back down

Don't forget your umbrella!

Water droplets or ice crystals form **raindrops** or **snowflakes**, which fall back to Earth.

6 It goes on and on

Rain and melted snow fill rivers, lakes and oceans, then the whole **water cycle** starts all over again. It helps create our weather.

How hot does it get?

In California's Death Valley, the top temperature ever recorded was over 56°C. A weather satellite has recorded over 70°C in the Lut Desert in Iran.

Where is the driest place on Earth?

The Atacama Desert in Chile. Once, no rain fell there for over 14 years. Long periods without rain are called droughts.

We can measure temperature in degrees Celsius (°C). At the centre of the Sun it's about 15 million°C

Why do lizards sunbathe?

Reptiles such as lizards are cold-blooded, which means that they can't make their own heat. They bask in the sunshine to warm themselves up.

Atacama Desert

Lizard

How can plants survive in a desert?

Some plants have their own water supply. Cacti store water in their thick, spiky stems. Baobab trees store water inside their big, fat trunks.

Cactus

Baobab tree

Why can the Sun be a danger?

The Sun can burn your skin and make you ill. On a sunny day, cover up your skin, wear a hat, slap on some sun cream and drink plenty of water.

Don't forget I need a drink too!

Where does the weather happen?

In the layer of the atmosphere that is closest to Earth's surface. The atmosphere surrounds our planet like a giant blanket, screening out some harmful rays that come from the Sun.

Atmosphere

Cumulonimbus

What is a weather system?

Huge masses of air that swirl over Earth's surface are called weather systems. High pressure systems press air down against the land. They bring drier, clearer weather. Low pressure systems bring mild or rainy weather. The border between two systems is called a front.

On TV, the weather is explained with maps and symbols.

Cirrus

Why do clouds have funny shapes?

Some clouds are white and puffy, some are thin and streaky. Some pile up like big dark towers, some form little blobs. Their shape depends on whether they are full of water droplets or ice crystals and how high up they are.

Mackerel sky

Some clouds look like dragons, castles or bears in the sky. What can you see up there?

Is there a pot of gold at the end of a rainbow?

Only in fairy tales! Rainbows are the most beautiful sights in the sky. Air has no colour, but when sunlight passes through rain or mist, the water droplets break up the light into an arc of shimmering colours.

Why does the wind blow?

Because as warm air rises, cold air whooshes in to take its place, and the wind blows! Some winds blow between land and sea. Some cross deserts and mountains. Others blow all the way around the planet.

Cold air

Warm air

Sycamore seeds

How does the wind help plants?

Many trees and flowering plants have seeds that are scattered by the wind. Dandelion seeds are light and fluffy, and float a long way. Sycamore seeds are like helicopter blades, spinning around.

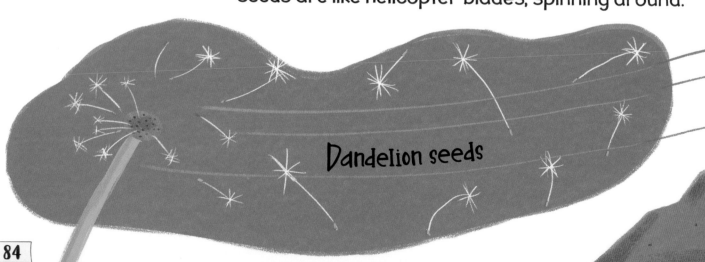

Dandelion seeds

What is the monsoon?

It is a wind that blows across India. The winter monsoon brings dry weather. In summer it picks up lots of water from the ocean and brings heavy rains to the dry land.

Summer monsoon can bring flooding.

Wandering albatross

Condor

Why do birds ride on the wind?

So we can fly long distances without too much flapping. Over the Southern Ocean, albatrosses like me glide on powerful winds. In South America, condors use currents of warm air to soar above mountains.

Pillar

How do winds shape rock?

Winds often carry dust, grit or sand. They blast rocks and cliffs, wearing them down into all sorts of shapes. Water, ice and heat also shape the surface of planet Earth.

Arch

Would you rather?

Go on holiday somewhere **cold** or somewhere **hot**?

Hear crashing **thunder** or see flashes of **lightning**?

BANG!

FLASH!

Play football in the **rain and mud** or during a **heatwave**?

Cruise by boat on a **calm day**...

...or sail on a **windy day**?

Fly **above** the clouds...

Sheep's wool contains lanolin, a grease that keeps out the rain.

Wear a **woolly coat** like a sheep, or a **green raincoat** like a tree frog?

I am covered in waterproof skin!

Ride on a **surfboard**...

...or a **snowboard**?

Work outside in a **big storm** at sea or inside designing a weather satellite for space?

...or drift **below** the clouds?

What is a hurricane?

It's a terrifying tropical storm, also called a typhoon or a cyclone. A great storm cloud spins around as it sweeps over the ocean. Hurricane-force winds can reach 180 kilometres an hour or even more.

The calm centre is called the 'eye' of the storm.

Is it deadly?

When a hurricane smashes into land it can be deadly. There are huge waves, heavy rain, floods and mudslides. Trees can be blown over, homes may be destroyed, and lives may be at risk.

Where is Tornado Alley?

This is an area in the United States that has some of the fiercest whirlwinds of all. They are called tornadoes or twisters. These dark funnels of dust can spin at up to 500 kilometres an hour. They can suck up a car or even a house.

WATCH OUT!

What is a waterspout?

A whirlwind that forms from warm, moist air over a sea or lake is called a waterspout. It is often joined to the bottom of a cloud.

Why are thunder clouds dark?

Thunder clouds are so full of water droplets that they look very dark. They tower up to 15 kilometres high.

How do clouds make lightning?

Water vapour rushes up into clouds from the warm ground. Once inside, the vapour cools and freezes, forming balls of ice called hailstones. Air currents ping these up and down inside the cloud, making an electric charge.

In a thunderstorm, stay away from water or metal fences.

BANG!

BOOM!

Thunderstorms can be dangerous.

Why does thunder go bang?

The heat of lightning is incredible, even hotter than the Sun. It makes the air expand so fast that it causes a shockwave. BANG!

Which comes first, thunder or lightning?

They happen at the same time, but we see the flash first because light travels through the air faster than sound.

How fast is lightning?

The electricity connects with the ground or with other clouds, forming a flash of lightning. This can travel 120,000 kilometres in a single second.

Go indoors if you can.

Do not stand under a tree.

Did you know?

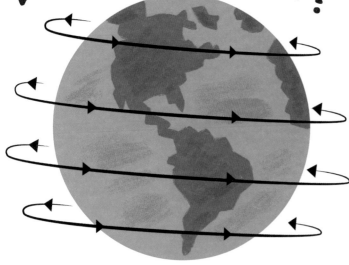

Super-powerful long-distance winds called **jet streams** rip along about 10 kilometres above the Earth's surface.

The Inuit people of the Arctic can build **igloos** — overnight shelters made from blocks of frozen snow. These are actually quite cosy!

It is said that no two **snowflakes** have exactly the same design!

Fog is just low-level cloud. The Grand Banks off Newfoundland, Canada, have about 206 foggy days each year.

As you are reading these words, there are about 2000 **thunderstorms** happening around the world.

The spinning of the Earth forces **winds** that blow from the Poles to the Equator to change direction.

COUGH!

When fumes from cars and factories react with sunlight, the air is filled with horrible, poisonous **smog**.

The coats of the **Arctic fox** and **hare** change to white in the winter, so they cannot be seen against the snow.

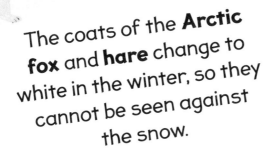

Fir trees have thin, tough leaves called **needles**, which stay on all winter. These help capture sunlight all year round. They can store water and survive harsh winter storms.

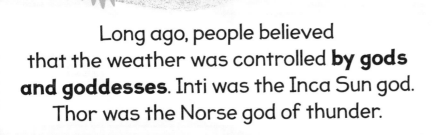

Long ago, people believed that the weather was controlled **by gods and goddesses**. Inti was the Inca Sun god. Thor was the Norse god of thunder.

How are snowflakes formed?

When water droplets freeze around specks of dust in a cloud, snowflakes form. These ice crystals freeze more droplets, building up amazing starry shapes and patterns. They stick together to make bigger flakes.

Snowflakes have SIX sides, or points.

What is a blizzard?

A blizzard is a heavy snow storm driven by high winds. Snow piles up in deep drifts. It's hard to see where you are going as everything looks white!

Why are mountaintops snowy?

Mountaintops are often covered in snow, even in hot countries. The higher you climb, the more the air expands and cools. This leads to more moisture — and snowy mountain conditions.

Where does frost make flowers?

On cold surfaces such as windows, ice or rock. Ice crystals spread into beautiful patterns, which look like ferns or flowers.

DANGER THIN ICE!

Does the sea ever freeze?

Yes it does, but because the sea contains salt, it has a lower freezing point. It turns to ice below -2° Celsius. Freshwater rivers and lakes freeze at 0° Celsius.

How many?

332
The number of days it once rained non-stop on the Hawaiian Island of Oahu!

4000
The number of hours of sunshine that Yuma, Arizona, USA receives in a year. It may be the sunniest place on Earth!

The biggest tropical storm ever recorded was a typhoon named Tip, in 1979. It measured **2220** kilometres across.

5 years!

That's how long a water-holding frog can go without water during a drought!

11.5 metres: The amount of snow that fell at Tamarack in California, USA, during just one day in 1911.

321
The number of kilometres a single lightning streak ran across the sky above Oklahoma, USA in 2007.

207
The number of tornadoes that happened in a single day in the USA in 2011.

8 hours **58** minutes:
The longest-lasting rainbow in Taiwan, in 2017.

1
The weight in kilograms of giant hailstones that fell in Bangladesh in 1986.

−89.2° Celsius.
The lowest temperature ever recorded was at the Vostok scientific base in Antarctica, in July 1983.

BRRRR!

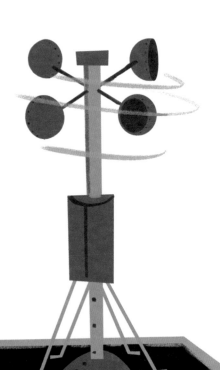

How do we measure the weather?

All sorts of clever gadgets have been invented over the years to measure how the weather behaves. Today, the numbers are often recorded and displayed digitally.

Anemometers measure wind speed. They are often fixed to tall buildings, bridges and ships.

Rain gauges collect and measure the amount of rain that falls into a jar.

Thermometers measure how hot or cold it gets. The best known thermometers show how a liquid metal called mercury goes up or down inside a glass tube. Most weather scientists today use electrical resistance thermometers.

Barometers measure changes in air pressure. There are many different designs and displays.

Satellites

Weather balloons carry instruments high above Earth to study the atmosphere.

Buoy

Satellites in space help us collect information about the climate. Buoys and ships at sea also record weather data, and so do aircraft.

Weather science is called meteorology.

Does the climate ever change?

Over millions of years, Earth's climate has gone through many changes. In the past there have been great ice ages, when ice spread out from the poles.

I lived in the ice age thousands of years ago.

Woolly mammoth

What's happening today?

The climate is changing very quickly. This is because we are cutting down forests and burning too much oil, gas and coal. We are filling the atmosphere with gases that make the planet overheat.

Solar panels use energy from the Sun to create electricity

Polar bear

Melting sea ice makes it hard for me to find food.

How will climate change affect the weather?

We may see more big tropical storms, floods in some places and droughts in others, melting ice and rising sea levels. Dry areas may turn to desert.

How can the weather help us out?

We can use wind, sunlight, waves, tides and rivers to make cleaner energy that never runs out. Let's look after our planet — it's the only one we've got!

Solar power

The wind turns turbines to make power for homes

Wind power

Hydroelectric power

Running water helps us create electricity too

A compendium of questions

Why is rain sometimes red?

If rain gets mixed with sand picked up by desert winds, it can be red or orange.

Hi, i'm Katrina!

Why are hurricanes given names?

It's an easy way of remembering which was which. Famous tropical storms have been called Katrina, Maria, Mitch and David.

Some of the sculptures are over 10 metres high!

Where is there a special snow festival?

It is held each year in Sapporo, Japan. People make amazing statues and sculptures from ice and snow.

Hello, I'm Mitch!

Why do crocodiles like tropical storms?

Flooding caused by hurricanes can make areas that crocodiles usually can't get to more accessible to them. So people may see them in unexpected places.

I'm off to the shops!

Why do people build houses on stilts?

When it floods in the rainy season in Assam, India, the houses stay high and dry.

People have to wade through flooded streets during monsoons.

Which countries have the worst floods?

India, Bangladesh and China have had some of the worst floods. This is due to heavy rains, melting snow from high mountains, big rivers and tropical storms.

Can it really rain frogs or fishes?

Yes! Tiny fish and frogs are sometimes sucked out of ponds and puddles by strong winds, then fall back to land when it rains.

Wheeeee eeeeee!

There have also been reports of rains of worms AND of tadpoles!

How do desert animals stay cool?

Many animals burrow underground and only come out at night, when it's cooler. The big ears of the fennec fox help its body to lose heat.

Hairs inside my ears help to keep out dust and sand.

Where are rivers used as roads?

Winters are so cold in Siberia, Russia, that heavy trucks can drive along frozen rivers instead of roads. Milk is sold in solid slabs.

The city of Yakutsk in Siberia is built on soil that is always frozen, even in summer!

Why is our planet in peril?

Our beautiful planet is in peril because we haven't been taking good care of it. Earth is a precious home for all of us, and the plants and animals that live here too.

How many people are on the planet?

There are more than 7.7 billion people. That's 7,700,000,000 humans! Every one of us has an important job to do. Let's work together to save the Earth!

What is air?

The air is made up of gases and it's wrapped around Earth like a snug blanket. It's called the atmosphere.

21% oxygen

78% nitrogen

1% other gases, including carbon dioxide

Humans breathe in oxygen and breathe out carbon dioxide.

A gas called nitrogen makes up most of the atmosphere. Which gas makes up the next biggest part of the atmosphere?

Plants' leaves take in carbon dioxide to make food. They give out oxygen.

Why does Earth need a blanket?

A blanket of air keeps our planet the perfect temperature!

① As the Sun's energy reaches Earth's atmosphere, some of it travels through and warms the surface

The gases in the atmosphere that trap the heat, such as carbon dioxide and methane, are called greenhouse gases.

② Earth's surface releases heat and some of it escapes back into space

③ Gases in the atmosphere trap some of the heat and reflect it back to Earth, keeping our planet a lovely warm place to live. This is called the greenhouse effect

Atmosphere

The world's oceans are warming up and melting my icy Arctic home.

Is Earth getting hotter?

Yes! Things humans do are creating more greenhouse gases. This means that more heat is trapped, so Earth is getting too warm. This is called global warming. Our weather is being affected – we call that climate change.

Did you know?

Carbon dioxide

Plants are great at mopping up extra carbon dioxide and pumping lots of oxygen into the air! That's why we need forests, fields and parks.

Oxygen

If we didn't have an atmosphere there would be no air to breathe, and Earth's average temperature would be a very chilly -6°C!

There are more than one billion cows in the world, and almost all of them are kept on farms. They all make greenhouse gases when they fart and burp.

Sometimes Earth is called the Goldilocks planet because its distance from the Sun means it's just the right temperature for us.

5000 TODAY!

You can plant a tree to help keep Earth's atmosphere healthy. Some trees are more than 5000 years old.

Too hot!

Just right!

Too cold!

Scientists looked at how hot the Earth was in the last 100 years and found the five hottest years have been since 2010.

Trees can be used to make all of these things: soap, shampoo, rubber gloves, chocolate, paper, clothes and medicines. When trees are cut down, it's important that new ones are planted.

Plants make perfect presents for people who care about the planet!

If you lined up all the cars in the world they could stretch round it 40 times! Think of all the dirty gases they are putting in the air, and leave your car at home whenever you can!

Trains are a greener way to travel than planes because they make up to six times less dirty gas.

We are taking too many fish from the sea. Some fishing nets are more than 60 metres wide and can trap tens of thousands of fish at a time.

What is dirty energy?

Burning oil, gas, wood and coal gives us energy to power our homes and vehicles. This puts more greenhouse gases in the air, and causes pollution.

Pollution is something in the environment that is harmful or poisonous.

Oil, gas and coal are called fossil fuels because they formed inside Earth long ago, from dead animals and plants!

Smoke containing harmful gases

This power station is burning coal. Most air pollution comes from burning fossil fuels

How can bikes help us save the planet?

Cycling, skate-boarding and walking are clean, green ways to get around. You can travel one kilometre by bike in about three minutes, by skateboard in about six minutes, or on foot in about 10 minutes.

This cycle lane is made up of solar panels. They use the Sun's energy to make electricity for lots of people.

Solar panels

What is clean energy?

Not all power comes from dirty fossil fuels. The great news is that there are loads of ways of making clean, green energy!

Wind turbines can turn wind energy into electricity, or other types of power

The energy of flowing water can be used to make hydroelectric power

Wind power

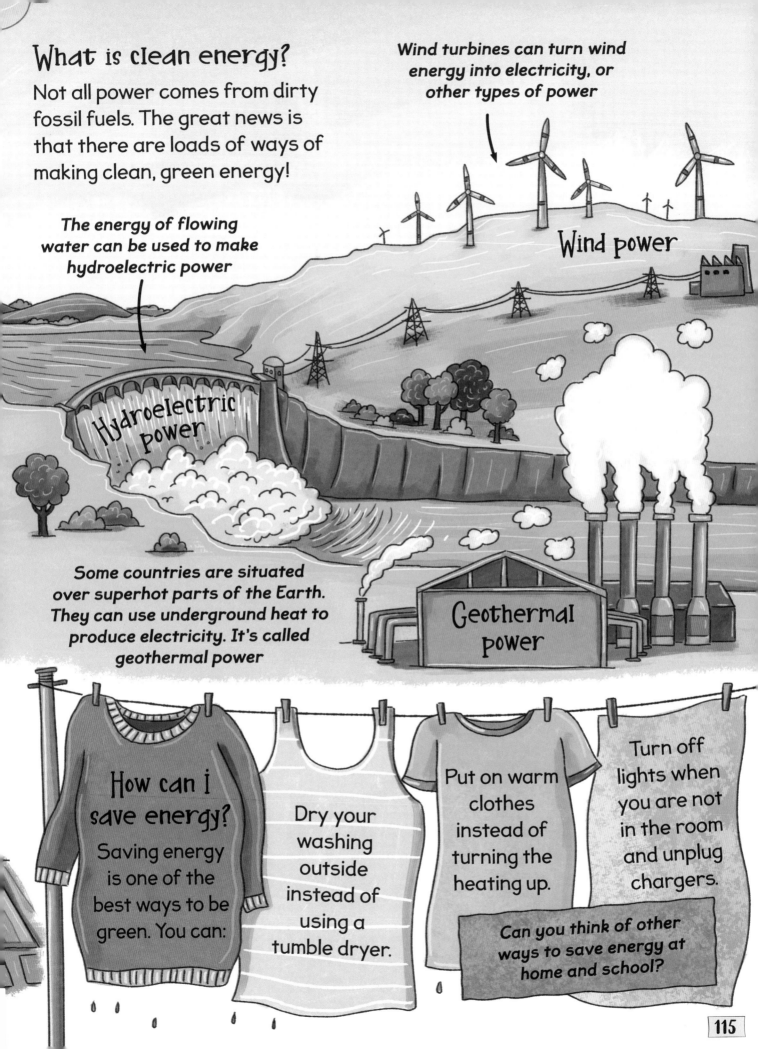

Hydroelectric power

Some countries are situated over superhot parts of the Earth. They can use underground heat to produce electricity. It's called geothermal power

Geothermal power

How can I save energy?

Saving energy is one of the best ways to be green. You can:

Dry your washing outside instead of using a tumble dryer.

Put on warm clothes instead of turning the heating up.

Turn off lights when you are not in the room and unplug chargers.

Can you think of other ways to save energy at home and school?

Why are jellyfish blooming?

Jellyfish love warm water, and as the world's oceans get warmer, the number of jellyfish is rising. Large numbers can even form massive groups, or blooms. The fish aren't so happy, as jellyfish eat them!

Seals that normally eat the fish now have less food. The damage we do to our planet affects all living things.

Why did my colourful home turn white?

Coral reefs need clean, warm water to survive. When the water gets too hot, or dirty, the coral animals die, and the reef turns white.

Why are the oceans dirty?

Our oceans are dirtier than ever because lots of plastic waste has been dumped in the water. Plastic in the ocean gets broken down into tiny pieces, and animals eat them.

How can I help turtles?

Some turtles try to eat plastic bags floating in the sea. They think the bags are their favourite food — jellyfish — and the plastic kills them.

Join a seaside clean-up to help keep beaches clean.

Always take your rubbish home and recycle as much of it as you can.

Ask for paper straws instead of plastic ones, which often end up in the sea.

You can help us turtles and other sea creatures by using canvas or long-life shopping bags instead of plastic ones.

When you go on holiday, don't buy souvenirs that are made from animals or their homes.

How many?

More than **80** countries already use wind power to produce electricity.

In Japan, people use wooden chopsticks to eat. Every year, they get through **90,000** tonnes of them! Can you think of some fun ways to reuse chopsticks?

1

The number of drinks cans you need to recycle to save energy for **4** hours of TV.

There is so much heat deep inside Earth that it could provide us with enough power for **1,000,000** years!

Make sure all your light bulbs are the new energy-saving ones. They last up to **15** times longer and can be recycled!

640

The number of litres of water a garden sprinkler uses in an hour. Use a watering can instead!

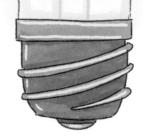

85% of the world's energy still comes from fossil fuels, although many people are working hard to reduce this. Are you?

100 The number of trees you could save from being cut down if your whole class recycle paper for a year.

It takes **50** times as much energy to make a battery as there is stored in the battery! Use rechargeable batteries whenever you can.

The Great Pacific Garbage Patch, a mass of litter floating in the North Pacific Ocean, covers around **1.6 million** square kilometres.

Pacific Ocean

10 The number of litres of clean water in a toilet flush.

Only **3%** of the water on Earth is fresh (not salty), and most of that is frozen. This is why we need to save water where we can.

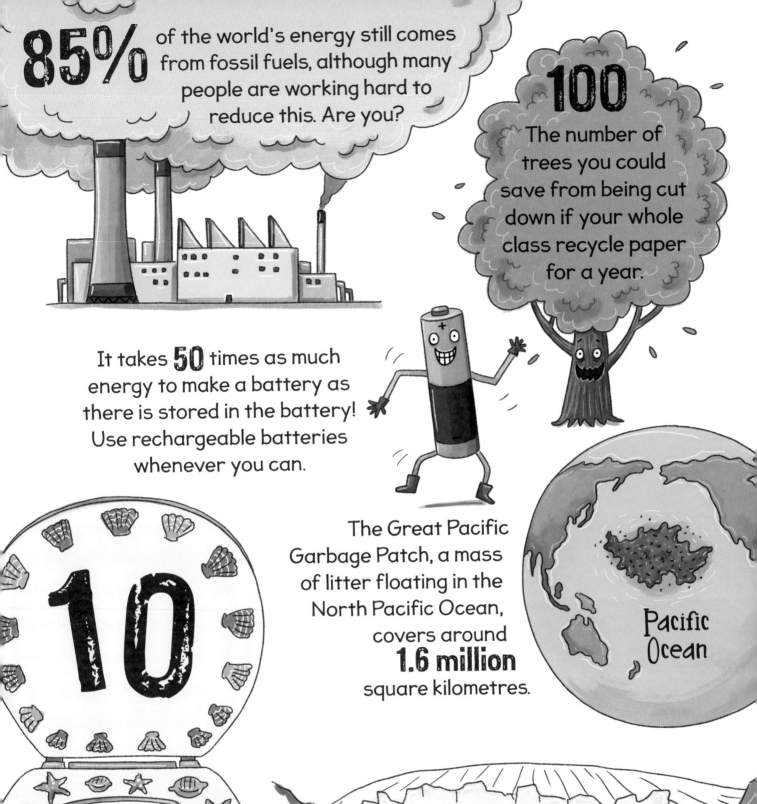

Where does wee go?

All of the waste water from our homes gets carried away in underground pipes. They're called sewers.

Why are showers best?

A bath uses about 80 litres of water, but a shower uses about 40 litres instead.

Cleaning water uses lots of energy. Turn off the tap while you are brushing your teeth. Can you think of other ways to save water?

That stinks!

Sewers carry the waste water to a place where it is cleaned so it can be used again

Some sewers also collect rainwater. If the sewer overflows, it empties into rivers or the ocean!

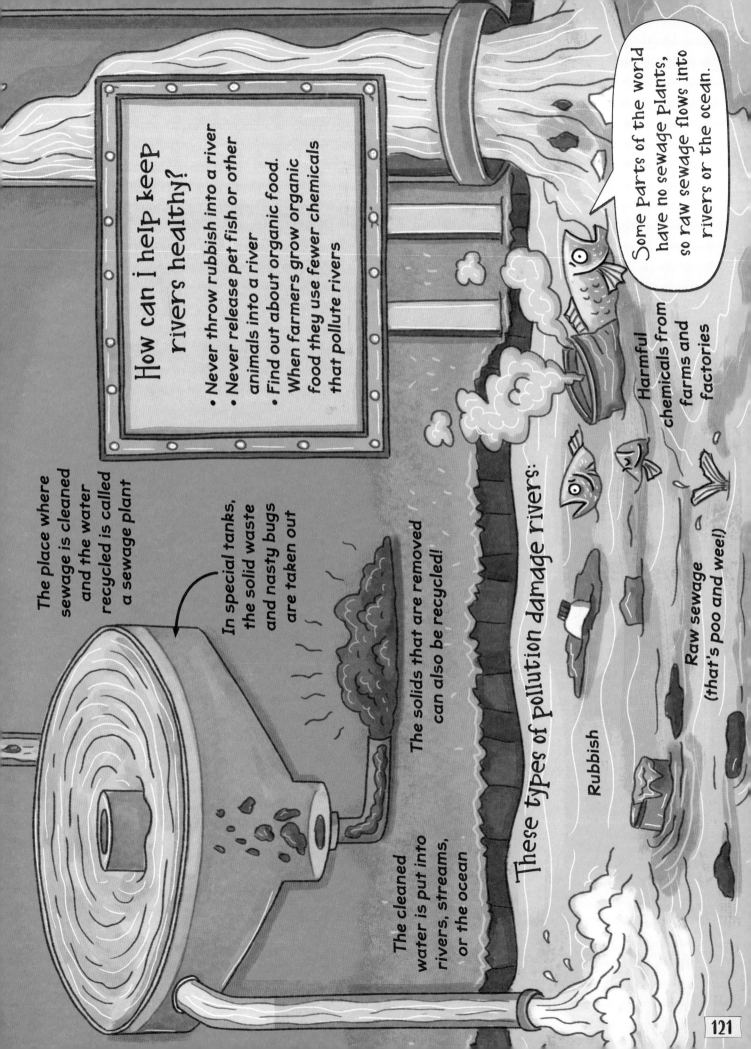

How can I help keep rivers healthy?

- Never throw rubbish into a river
- Never release pet fish or other animals into a river
- Find out about organic food. When farmers grow organic food they use fewer chemicals that pollute rivers

The place where sewage is cleaned and the water recycled is called a sewage plant

In special tanks, the solid waste and nasty bugs are taken out

The solids that are removed can also be recycled!

The cleaned water is put into rivers, streams, or the ocean

These types of pollution damage rivers:

Rubbish

Harmful chemicals from farms and factories

Raw sewage (that's poo and wee!)

Some parts of the world have no sewage plants, so raw sewage flows into rivers or the ocean.

How far did my banana travel?

The distance food travels from where it was grown, to where it will be eaten, is measured in food miles.

1

This banana travelled by truck to get to a boat

50 miles

2

Then it crossed an ocean

5000 miles

3

Then it was put on a lorry and taken to a supermarket

70 miles

4

We bought it and it travelled in our car to get to our home

5 miles

5

It came with me on my bike to school

How many food miles does this banana have? Which part of its journey used the least energy?

2 miles

How can food waste be turned into energy?

When food rots it gives off methane. This can be collected and used for cooking, or heating homes. Plant waste can also be used to make fuel for cars.

4 The methane is used to power electricity generators

5 Electricity is supplied to homes

3 Bacteria in the tank eat the waste, which gives off methane as it breaks down

Methane can also be collected from my poo!

1 Food waste is collected from homes, supermarkets and restaurants

2 All the waste goes in a special sealed tank, where no oxygen can reach it

Who has green fingers?

i do! i grow fruit and veg in my garden so these foods have no food miles!

i put the compost on my garden to help new plants grow. Thanks worms!

Why are worms really useful?

We munch up leftover food, peelings, eggshells and garden waste. We turn it into compost.

123

Would you rather?

Would you rather save water by sharing a **bath** with your dog, or by giving yourself a time limit on your **showers**?

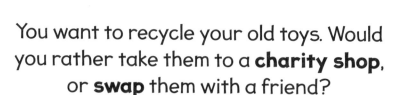

You want to recycle your old toys. Would you rather take them to a **charity shop**, or **swap** them with a friend?

If you get cold, would you rather warm up by **running** on the spot or by wearing a big **jumper**?

Would you rather be a wriggly worm eating **rotten food** in a compost heap, or a dung beetle munching on **elephant poo**?

Would you rather try to make a **space rocket** from cans, or a **submarine** from a plastic bottle?

If you worked in a safari park, would you rather **teach** people about nature... or **check** a crocodile's teeth?

You want to cut down your food miles. Would you rather catch your own **fish**, keep your own **hens**, or grow your own **tomatoes**?

Which environment would you most like to work to protect — the **Amazon rainforest** or the chilly **North Pole**?

What is an animal's home called?

The place where an animal lives is called a habitat. Forests, grasslands, rivers and deserts are types of habitat. When habitats are destroyed, some animals lose their homes, and might go extinct.

Bornean orang-utan

Where did your home go?

In Borneo, diverse forests the size of 180 football pitches are cut down every hour so palm trees can be grown. Avoid buying foods made with palm oil and you can help us keep our homes.

Bengal tiger

How can you help to save animal habitats?

Wildlife charities work to save habitats, and raising money for them is a good way to help. It's also a good idea to only buy food and products that have been made without harming wild habitats.

I'm doing a sponsored silence to raise money to protect wild habitats.

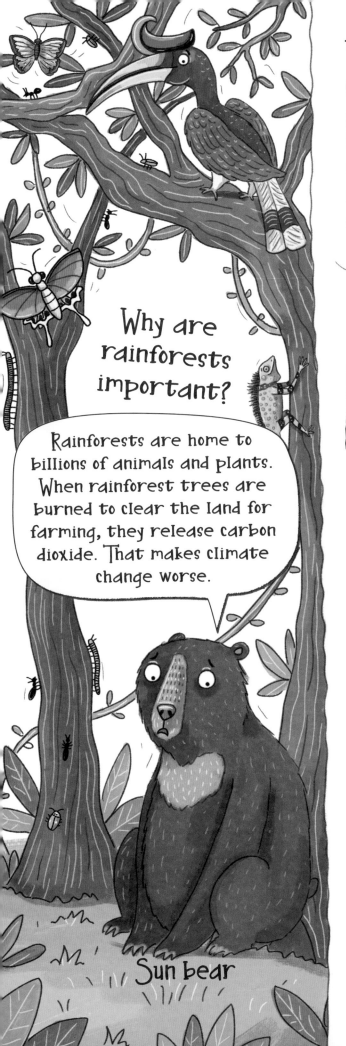

Why are rainforests important?

Rainforests are home to billions of animals and plants. When rainforest trees are burned to clear the land for farming, they release carbon dioxide. That makes climate change worse.

Sun bear

What causes extinction?

Extinction is when a type of animal or plant dies out so there are none left on Earth. There are lots of reasons for extinction, but today humans are doing so much damage to the world that we are putting many animals at risk.

Going...
Beluga sturgeons are under threat because they are fished for their valuable eggs

Going...
Rhinos are hunted and killed because some people want their horns

Gone
Golden toads probably went extinct because of global warming

Where does all the rubbish go?

When we throw rubbish away we sort it into different bins. Some of it will end up in landfill or being burned, which is very bad for the environment. It's better to go zero! That means trying to create no rubbish at all.

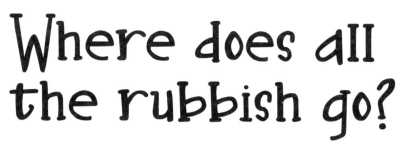

Painted turtles

Some of this rubbish will never rot. It will stay in the ground for hundreds, or even thousands of years.

What's that stink?

A landfill is a huge hole in the ground where rubbish is put. As the rubbish rots, it gives off methane. It's a more harmful greenhouse gas than carbon dioxide.

Grasshopper sparrow

Osprey

How can rubbish turn green?

Freshkills, in the USA, was once the world's biggest landfill. Now it's being turned into a park and more than 200 types of animal live there.

Why is rubbish a hot topic?

This rubbish is hot — burning hot! It's being burned in a big oven, called an incinerator. The rubbish is burned instead of being put into landfill. As it burns, it releases lots of pollution.

Five hundred steel cans can be recycled to build a bike!

How can I go zero?

If you recycle, or reuse, all your rubbish you have gone zero! Turn the page to discover how recycling and reusing helps to reduce the amount of rubbish that goes to landfill, or is burned.

129

What are the three Rs?

Reduce, Reuse and Recycle! By cutting down the amount of energy we use and waste we create, we can help to make Earth a better place.

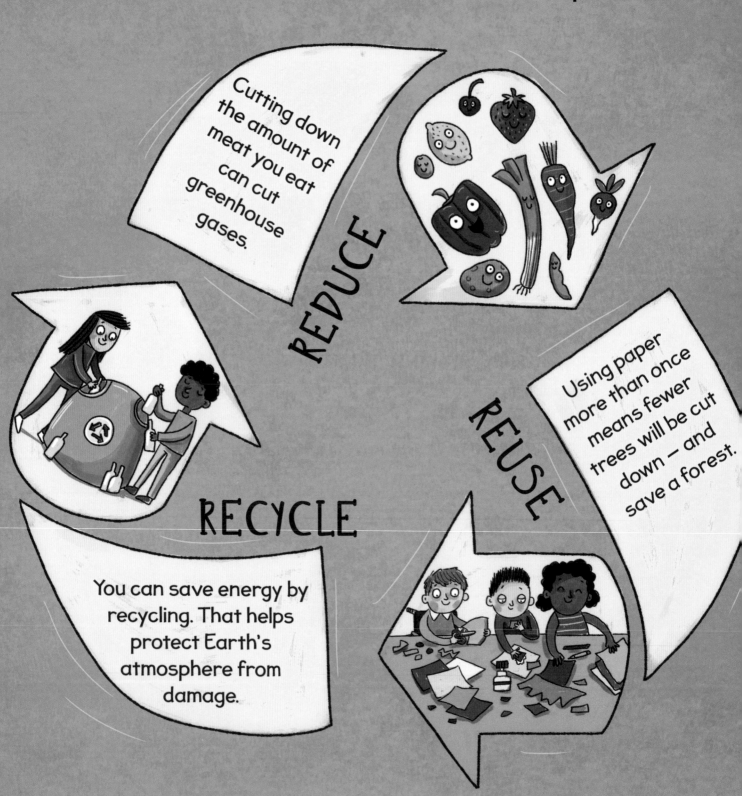

REDUCE

Cutting down the amount of meat you eat can cut greenhouse gases.

REUSE

Using paper more than once means fewer trees will be cut down – and save a forest.

RECYCLE

You can save energy by recycling. That helps protect Earth's atmosphere from damage.

Can poo be recycled?

Yes it can!

Elephant, rhino and kangaroo poo can be used to make paper

Llama poo can be burned on fires to keep people warm, or cook their food

The solid sludge that is collected at sewage farms can be turned into fertiliser. Farmers put it on their fields to help plants grow

How can we create less rubbish?

Plastic can be difficult to recycle, so try not to buy things that come in lots of plastic packaging.

Use a reusable water bottle and fill it with tap water.

Carry your lunch in reusable tubs or beeswax wrappers instead of plastic wrap.

Use a toothbrush made from bamboo, not plastic.

131

What are we doing to save the planet?

All over the world, people are working hard to save the planet for your future – at home, on farms and in the workplace. Saving the planet is a job for everyone.

What is conservation?
Conservation is the work people do to protect wild and special places.

What's a solar farm?

A solar farm is a place with lots of solar panels. The panels collect sunlight and turn it into electricity.

The largest solar farms are in hot countries. They have more than 2 million solar panels.

I'm a solar-powered cleaning machine! At this solar farm in India, we keep the panels clear of sand so they can keep soaking up the sunlight.

I live in the Amazon rainforest. I take care of this precious habitat so it will still be here for my children and grandchildren.

I'm in Antarctica, counting penguins to see how healthy this colony is.

We can all do our part to help save the Earth!

A compendium of questions

How can i use less plastic?
Think about whether you need to buy a product in plastic. Liquid soap, for example, comes in plastic bottles, but a bar of soap is wrapped in paper.

How many tigers are in the wild?

There are only around 3900 tigers left in the world. Recently, conservation work has been able to stop their numbers from falling, but they still need our protection to live safely in the wild.

How can I feed wild birds?

The easiest way to feed wild birds is to grow lots of flowers that will make seeds for the birds to eat in winter. You can also buy bird food and hang it from trees in bird feeders.

It's a good idea to fill up a bird bath, or leave a bowl of water out so birds can drink and wash — far from any place where cats can hide!

What can I do for nature on a day out?

Enjoy looking at plants and animals, but avoid picking flowers or disturbing animal homes. Always take your rubbish home.

Flowers make bees happy!

What should I do with old clothes?

Clothes can be recycled, they can be cut up and used as rags for cleaning, or if they are in good condition you can sell or swap them, or take them to charity shops.

Can I make gifts instead of buying them?

Making gifts is a great way to reuse and recycle. You could turn old greetings cards into bookmarks and gift tags.

It's fun to make things, and now these cards won't be thrown away!

GLUE

What's a swap-shop?

Instead of throwing things out, you can swap them! Set up a swap-shop where people can bring toys or books they have finished using, and trade them for something someone else has donated.

You could set up a swap-shop like this one at school.

What type of gift keeps on giving?

A plant! You can grow a tomato or bean plant from seed and give it to someone else.

What is a carbon footprint?

It is a measure of how much carbon dioxide is released into the atmosphere because of how you live your life. Cutting our carbon footprint will help in the battle against climate change.

How can I make an animal habitat?

Make a pile of logs, sticks and leaves in a shady place outside. Soon all sorts of bugs and small animals will be happy to make their home there.

index

Page numbers in *italics* refer to pages having only pictures of items.